# Palladian Bridges

*Prior Park and the Whig Connection*

*Cover illustration: the north face of the bridge at Prior Park
(photograph by Joshua Briggs who also took
the colour photographs on pp 19–21)*

*This Thomas Robins sketch shows the Prior Park bridge in 1758, approached by one of the serpentine paths of the earliest Rococo garden layout. The bridge composes as the foreground to a picturesque landscape with Widcombe church, the Manor, its garden house and Widcombe Hill House in the background (Conway Library, Courtauld Institute of Art)*

# Palladian Bridges

*Prior Park and the Whig Connection*

Tim Mowl

*For ~~Bob~~ and Michael,
with affections,
from their friend,
the author,*

6 · ix · '93

**Millstream Books
in association with
Bath Preservation Trust**

First published 1993
Millstream Books
7 Orange Grove
Bath BA1 1LP

Typeset by Ryburn Publishing Services, Keele University
Printed in Great Britain by The Matthews Wright Press, Chard

ISBN 0948975342

## Two Trusts and Prior Park

In 1936 the Bath Preservation Trust sent an architect member, Mowbray Green, F.R.I.B.A., to report on the state of the Prior Park bridge and make recommendations as to its repair. With the help of the Mayor's Fund the bridge and the weirs were repaired, and a new sluice gate raised the water of the lake to its original level. In recognition of their contribution, Prior Park School allowed members of the Bath Preservation Trust a master ticket enabling them to visit the bridge at all times by way of the lane leading from Widcombe Old Church.

The National Trust has now undertaken the restoration of Prior Park's grounds and the Bath Preservation Trust will continue to make the Palladian bridge its particular responsibility. This book has been sponsored by the Bath Preservation Trust and proceeds from its sale will go towards the repair of the bridge.

Michael Briggs
Chairman
Bath Preservation Trust
Spring 1993

# Preface

A few years back, when I was writing a weekly article on architectural and environmental matters for the Bath *Evening Chronicle*, I spent a whole enthusiastic column of print in praise of the gently crumbling stonework of the Prior Park Palladian bridge and the unkempt inaccessibility of its reedy lake. The place was pure poetry on the doorstep of suburban Bath. Its essential charm then lay in its forlorn neglect and loosely guarded isolation. So there is irony now in my writing a book about the same bridge that may well be sold at a kiosk as the public gain legitimate entry to a landscape that was once enjoyably private.

That, of course, is the dilemma at the heart of the Heritage industry and the problem that the National Trust faces every time it takes over a property of intensely individual character and applies institutional methods to its upkeep. Ideally this bridge should be appreciated when you are alone some summer's evening. A butler should be bringing down a cold collation from the palace up the hill for you to eat on the lake shore as a string quartet plays from the bridge itself. The surface of the water and the temple vault together would create a confused acoustic and you could lose yourself in a pleasing melancholy.

In fact Prior Park has rarely offered such ideal opportunities to its best known monument. Ralph Allen built the bridge as a gesture of political solidarity with the ruling government and was, in any case, a notably prosaic fellow. When he died his dreadful niece inherited it, surely the stuffiest and least deserving heiress of the whole 18th century. No poets seem ever to have languished by the lakeside nor gallants courted in its temple's shade. How the bridge featured when Prior Park was a seminary and the Corpus Christi masses were celebrated on the terraces above is not known. That 19th-century convert and Jesuit, Gerald Manley Hopkins, would have raptured over the site, but he never came here.

What the bridge and lake now need is a union of watchful neglect and inspired access. May the weeds still grow a little and the lawn mower approach only once a year. But when the weather forecasts seem settled and nights are warm, the Bath Preservation Trust, which has kept a sixty-year guard on the bridge, could sponsor open air concerts. Bath has always been the place for polite revels, for Monteverdi and Mozart by moonlight. And if the National Trust cannot guarantee that there will be fireflies and nightingales it can, at least, by leaving slopes of deep grass and untrimmed thickets, encourage such background *son et lumière*. With vision the best may yet be to come.

I should like to thank the Chairman and trustees of the Bath Preservation Trust for inviting me to write about these bridges, but particularly Gillian Sladen who has given both scholarly and enthusiastic support. Thanks also to: Dianne Barre; Reg and Maureen Barton; Joshua Briggs for superb colour photography; Brian Earnshaw; Oliver Garnett; John Harris; Peter Hayden; Gervase Jackson-Stops; Gordon Kelsey; Tim Knox; Andrew Norris; John Phibbs; Christopher Woodward. Finally my thanks to our publisher, Tim Graham, who has guided the book through to publication with his customary enthusiasm and efficiency.

Tim Mowl
Cotham
Bristol
Spring 1993

REGINA VIRTUS

THE THIRD BOOK OF
ARCHITECTURE
by
ANDREA PALLADIO
WHEREIN
the WAYS, BRIDGES, PIAZZAS, BASILICAS,
and XISTI are treated of.

LONDON,
Published by
ISAAC WARE,
Anno MDCCXXXVIII.

*Isaac Ware adapted Palladio's original frontispiece to the Third Book, retaining its Mannerist strapwork and broken pediment*

If there was any justice in vocabulary then bridges such as that across the lake in the combe below Prior Park would not be called 'Palladian' but 'Herbertian', and if that sounds unsuitably irreverent then 'Wiltonian' or 'Pembrokian' might serve. The prototype templar crossing was devised in 1736 or 1737 by Henry Herbert, 9th Earl of Pembroke (1689–1750), to bridge the Nadder in the garden of his Wiltshire seat, Wilton House. The Earl had more than a little help over the design from his architectural collaborator Roger Morris (1695–1749), but 'Morrissian' is no more euphonious than Herbertian so the traditional Palladian attribution will have to stand. Both the Earl and Roger Morris were, in fact, enthusiasts for the pure classical style of building that had been developed around Venice and Vicenza in the middle decades of the 16th century by Andrea Palladio (1508–1580) and carried on by his disciple Vincenzo Scamozzi (1552–1616). There is something of all four men in the sprightly assurance of the Wilton Palladian bridge but a drawing of it in the library of Windsor Castle is actually signed 'R. Morris' and Morris was described as its 'Architect' on a plate of the bridge published in the *Vitruvius Britannicus* of 1771. John Devall, a stonemason, was responsible for the construction of the bridge. A keystone carries his initials J D and the date 1737.

## The true Palladian bridges

It is unlikely that Andrea Palladio would have approved of these playful, anything but functional, structures that have been named after him. Where bridges were concerned Palladio was an engineer with a puritan feeling for the satisfying beauty of a functional structure. As an architect of villas, churches and public buildings he designed with an austere concern for what he believed, probably wrongly, to have been the pure Vitruvian classicism of the Rome of Augustus. This was while most of his contemporaries in Italy were indulging themselves with a Mannerist classicism that played with and distorted those antique forms.

In *I Quattro Libri dell' Architettura*, which he published in Venice in 1570 to sum up his ideals and his life's work, Palladio devoted more than half its Third Book, the section 'wherein the Ways, Bridges, Piazzas, Basilicas and Xisti are treated of', to bridges. They take up eleven of its twenty-one plates. He covers three types – wooden bridges, ordinary stone bridges and one extraordinary Aelian or monumental bridge with loggias. In its Italian editions the *Quattro Libri* was familiar to English architects and enthusiasts of the 17th century. After the publication of an English translation by Giacomo Leoni in 1715 and another by Isaac Ware in 1738

9

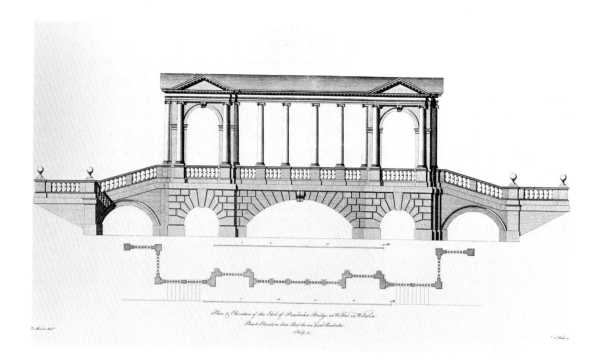

Plan & Elevation of the Earl of Pembroke's Bridge at Wilton in Wiltshire.
Plan & Elevation d'un Pont du mi Lord Pembroke.

*The Four Books of Andrea Palladio's Architecture* became accessible to a much wider public in this country. Thereafter, to the average improver of an 18th-century park, all three distinct and very different bridge types discussed in the Third Book – wooden, stone and monumental – were classed equally as 'Palladian'. In fact only the wooden and plain stone bridges built as English park features were exact copies of Palladio's plates. The monumental bridge with a temple-style loggia, like that at Prior Park, was an inspired improvisation by Lord Pembroke, or Morris, using elements from Plate 9 in the Third Book but in the spirit of a much livelier, less magisterial, bridge on a drawing by Vincenzo Scamozzi which had found its way into Lord Burlington's collection. It is probable that this Scamozzi drawing had originally belonged to Inigo Jones (1573–1652) as the great Caroline architect had met Scamozzi during a visit he made to Italy in 1613–14 to collect drawings by Palladio.

After 1719 Lord Burlington saw it as his mission to revive in England the pure classical forms of Palladio, Scamozzi and Jones. It was chiefly due to his patronage that Palladianism became virtually the house-style of the Whig aristocrats in the decades of their political ascendancy from 1714 to 1760. The Earl of Pembroke was a Whig and second only to Lord Burlington as a gifted architectural amateur in the revived Palladian. Indeed Horace Walpole rated Pembroke above either Burlington or William Kent.

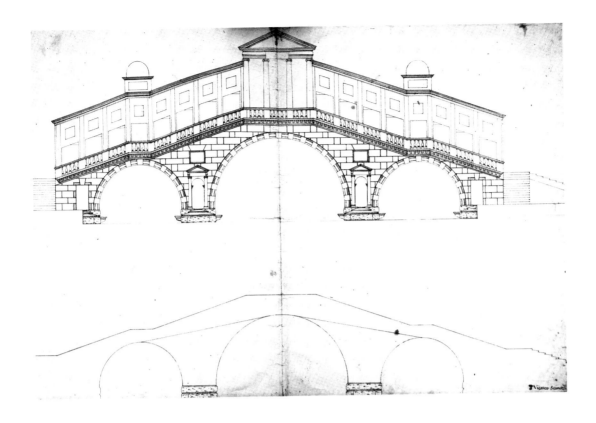

## 'Strong, beautiful and commodious' – the Palladian bridge in wood

Quite apart from the visual satisfaction which a wooden bridge offered through its open display of structural geometry, Palladio was drawn to such solutions through the historical precedent of the great wooden bridge, 'an admirable work, and most difficult by reason of the breadth, height and rapidity of the river', that Julius Caesar had thrown across the Rhine. The only loggiaed, and in a rustic sense monumental, bridge that Palladio himself ever actually built rather than drew was a superior version of Caesar's bridge that he designed to cross the fast-flowing Brenta at Bassano del Grappa, an Italian town at the foot of the Alps. Though several times destroyed by floods or war, the bridge at Bassano has always been rebuilt in something close to its original Palladian form with five spans on 'four orders of piles' set so that 'by how much greater the strength of the water was, so much the firmer the whole kept braced together'. The roadway across it runs level and protected from snowfalls by a roof supported on twin rows of wooden Doric columns that 'serve as a loggia, and make the whole work very commodious and beautiful'.

11

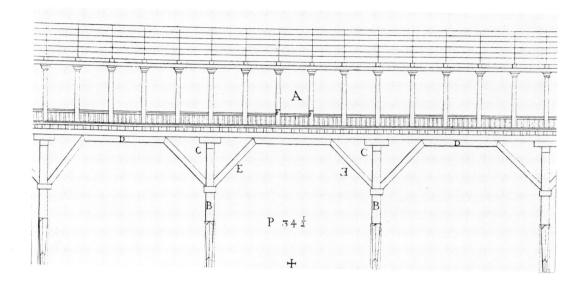

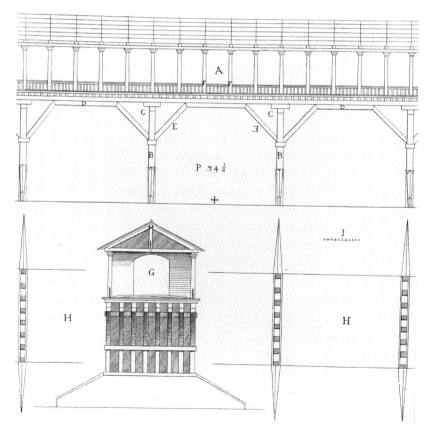

*Palladio's design for the bridge that he built across the Brenta at Bassano del Grappa*

This bridge at Bassano never inspired an English imitation. It was a more severely functional Palladian original, an 'Invention, according to which wooden bridges may be made, without fixing

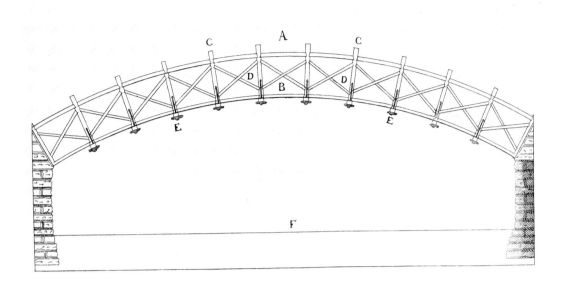

any posts in the water' that took the fancy of the English aristocracy and royalty. In part the economy and ingenuity of Palladio's 'Invention' were the attraction, but there is no doubt, from contemporary comment, that these bridges, particularly the version illustrated in Plate 5, that rises in a high jaunty arc above the water, were seen as Chinese in outline and readily convertible into set pieces of picturesque Chinoiserie by a little readjustment of the braces that fence and support the main side posts or 'colonelli' of their walkways. Palladio had appreciated how readily his design could be adapted to the width of a stream provided that the height of the bridge 'be an eleventh part of the breadth of the river'. That lively curve was essential to its structural soundness; the 'Chinese' angularity was merely incidental.

*Plate 5 of Palladio's Third Book of Architecture – the Italian source of so many later 'Chinese' bridges in English parks*

## 'Of more glory to the builders'
## – Palladio's stone prototypes

In his non-monumental stone bridges Palladio made no effort to innovate. He was content to illustrate and imitate the many Roman examples that still survived in his lifetime up and down the Italian peninsula. He insisted only on an even number of piers and therefore an odd number of arches. His favourite, as illustrated on

13

*Plate 7 of the Third Book – the Roman bridge at Rimini*

Plate 7, was one built, he supposed, by Augustus at Rimini with five arches, the middle three wider and higher than the flanking pair, its cutwaters right-angled to face the current and topped with tabernacles for statues and a final cornice. Plate 11 of the Third Book illustrates a three-arched version of that Roman original which Palladio designed for 'some gentlemen' but never built. When the Northamptonshire mason, Thomas Grumbold of Great Weldon, was asked to design an ornamental bridge across the Cam at Cambridge leading to Clare College, he seems to have produced a deliberate and very successful version of Plate 11, complete with ornate statuary and a cornice. Clare's bridge has therefore a good claim to be the first Palladian bridge in England, the only mystery being why such an expensive and massively ornamental structure came to be built while the college itself was only half complete. The bridge was in place before 1640 – Cambridge's aesthetic answer to Oxford's Canterbury Quad at St John's College and a sign of the stylistic sophistication of University Common Rooms in the years before the Civil War. No link

*Plate 11 of the Third Book, probably the inspiration for Thomas Grumbold's bridge at Clare College, Cambridge*

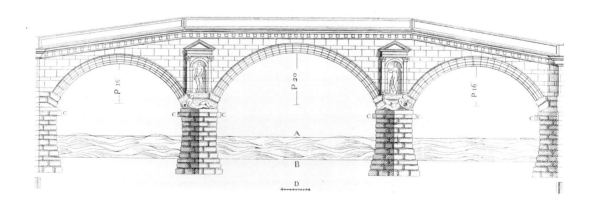

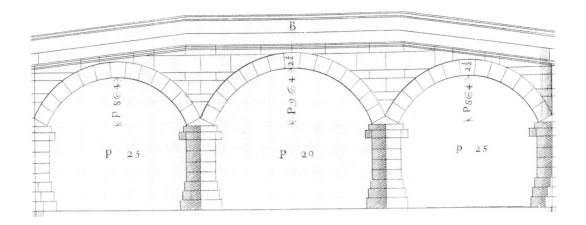

between the bridge at Clare and Inigo Jones has ever been established, but Jones was never content simply to imitate an original design by Palladio and the balustraded parapet of the Clare bridge is a Scamozzian touch that could well have been suggested by Jones. The humorous carved panels over the cutwaters at Clare appear to have been inspired by the river nymphs on Palladio's Plate 11. Only the engaging dip in the roadway above the central arch is purely 17th-century English.

*Plate 12 of the Third Book*

## Palladio's 'Stone Bridge of my invention' – the first of the two Wilton sources

The bridge that Palladio designed, in competition with Sansovino and Michelangelo, to cross the Grand Canal in Venice at the Rialto was both grandiose and classically correct in the Vitruvian sense. It was to be a three-arched palace rather than a bridge and so loaded with templar structures that his drawings could have been quarried to devise far more than the one bridge that Lord Pembroke and Roger Morris contrived. Though he never mentions Venice in his text, Palladio was designing a structure both functional and prestigious for 'the metropolis of many other cities … where there is a very great traffick carried on, almost from every part of the world'. It was to carry 72 shops on three streets:

> *… that in the middle, ample and beautiful, and the other two, one on each side, somewhat less. On each side of these streets I ordered shops, so that there would have been six rows of them. Besides this, in the heads of the bridge, and in the middle, that is upon the greatest arch, I made loggia's, in which the merchants might have assembled to negotiate together; and it would have afforded conveniency and very great beauty.*

15

*Elements of the English Palladian bridge are apparent in the left-hand arch and loggia of the bridge that Palladio hoped to build across the Grand Canal in Venice*

When appraising the English Palladian bridges it is important to remember this concept of airy rooms, meeting places suspended over water. They were not meant simply as ornamental passages from one bank to another but as alfresco living rooms. Palladio protested that he was only following a Roman precedent. The Pons Aelius leading over the Tiber to the Mausoleum of Hadrian was, in its prime, 'covered over with loggia's, with columns of bronzo, with statues and with other curious ornaments'. To emphasise the functional seriousness of his project, 'and also to add a very great income to it', he drew on Plate 9 the exterior of the shops as they would appear from a canal boat and, on Plate 10, the street fronts of the shops as customers would see them from the streets. The bridge was level but reached by a flight of steps from each end – a detail Sir John Vanbrugh seems only half to have noted.

In the event Palladio's design was rejected and the existing bold but relatively simple Rialto bridge was the creation of Giovanni da Ponte. So it came about that the outside elevation of a row of shops intended to stress Venice's role as the natural heir of Rome was only realised as a favourite park ornament for 18th-century English gentry of a certain political persuasion, who may well have seen themselves as a northern version of Venice's controlling oligarchy.

16

View of y Bridge of Blenheim                    Veue du Pont de Blenheim du Côte de la Ville

AA  The Great Arch Opens·                    Feet 100
BB  The hollow of the Bridge with Grotts &c.
C   The Length of the Bridge                       400
D   The Breadth of the same                         60
E   The Breadth over the great Arch                 40
F   Its hight from the Water to the Top             80

AA  L'Etendüe du Grand Arc                     Ped    1
BB  l'uide du Pont ou il y a des Grottes et des Fontains
C   La Longeur du Pont                              4
D   La Largeur
E   La Largeur Sur le Grand Arc
F   La Hauteur du mesme Pont

## 'As for the Bridge I do love it'
## – Vanbrugh's version of Palladio's Rialto project

*The imperial viaduct which Vanbrugh devised to dignify the park at Blenheim was never completed with its twin temples, loggia and gargantuan urns*

Sir John Vanbrugh (1664–1726) was far too original an architect ever to be a strict Palladian but here and there under the imaginative skylines of his palaces and on their gouty, baroque façades he drops heavy hints of Palladian awareness. It was typical of Vanbrugh that when, in April 1706, he offered a design for a park ornament at Blenheim in competition with Hawksmoor, Wise and Wren, he should have improvised on the grandest of Palladio's bridge projects, that for the Rialto. He knew, better than his competitors, the Duke of Marlborough's concept of the nature and purpose of Blenheim Palace and its surrounds. 'Tho' ordered to be a Dwelling house for the Duke of Marlborough and his posterity', Vanbrugh wrote, it was 'at the Same time by all the World looked on as a Publick Edifice, raised for a Monument of the Queen's Glory through his great Genius'. So Vanbrugh created a monumental design and a stone model, not for a bridge in any normal sense, but for an imperial viaduct, and won the competition.

Work on what the angry Duchess of Marlborough was to call 'the bridge in the air' began in June 1706 with Bartholomew Peisley as its contracting mason. The great central arch was raised by 1710 when the Duchess stopped the works. More was done between 1711 and 1716, in which year Vanbrugh was dismissed. By that time the bridge had achieved its present puzzling but wonderfully suggestive outlines. It stood then fifteen feet higher than it does today because it straddled a marshy valley and three branches of the diminutive Glym, not Capability Brown's splendid lake, created between 1764 and 1774.

17

*Flooded when Lancelot
Brown created the lake,
Vanbrugh's bridge lost
its basement stage but
gained a function
(Joshua Briggs)*

If the Blenheim bridge had been completed to Vanbrugh's original design its kinship with Palladio's bridge for the Rialto would have been more apparent. The 200-foot span of its central arch should have been topped by a double colonnade of 13 round arches, each colonnade ending in a temple with a pyramidal roof, a clear reference to Palladio's rows of shops and his bourse for merchants. While it could not, like Palladio's 100-foot wide giant, accommodate three streets it was, at 400 feet, almost twice as long. Until the massive earthworks needed to carry an approach road to the palace from the north were completed in 1720 it stood in strange dysfunctional isolation. Possibly Vanbrugh had intended it to be mounted by a flight of steps as Palladio's bridge was to have been; certainly the north drive to the Ditchley gate was rarely used and Vanbrugh must have realised that the Palace's main approach would always be from Oxford and Woodstock, to the south and east.

His bridge contains no less than 33 rooms, some of them now permanently under water. Within the north pier was housed Robert Aldersea's paddle engine to pump water up from the Glym to the palace. How the other rooms were to have been utilised is not clear but some have fireplaces and chimneys. Vanbrugh once laughingly assured the Duchess that 'if at last, there is a house found in that Bridge your Grace will go and live in it'. It is more probable that he was preparing a kind of grace and favour *pied-à-terre* for his own old age, somewhere with an oblique view of the Palace itself, his crowning masterpiece. For several years he had been furtively repairing the ruinous old manor house of Woodstock at the north end of the new bridge with some such a view in mind. His surname, as Kerry Downes has observed, means 'of the bridge' and a three-arched bridge featured on his coat of arms, so the whole structure should probably be seen as a piece of outrageous self-indulgence.

*The Palladian bridge at Wilton, 1737 (Joshua Briggs)*

*The Palladian bridge at Stowe, 1739 (Joshua Briggs)*

*The Palladian bridge at Prior Park, 1755 (Joshua Briggs)*

*The Palladian bridge at Tsarskoe Selo, 1771 (Peter Hayden)*

In the detail of its decoration Vanbrugh's bridge makes only token reference to conventional Palladian forms. Its cornice is corbelled out massively enough to support a pathway. The dripstones over its windows have a nightmare heaviness and the keystones of the central arch project with an almost Art Deco geometry to join the parapet. Palladio himself would have enjoyed its scale, deplored its detail and regretted its lack of function. Eventually, in 1730–1, a fluted Doric column crowned with a lead statue of the Duke was erected on its axis to the north, giving the bridge at least a visual purpose. The designer of the column was Lord Herbert, soon to be the 9th Earl of Pembroke and creator of an infinitely more acceptable Palladian model. As usual he was assisted in the design work by Roger Morris and the marble for the base of the column was supplied by another young architect later to be much associated with the design of a very different kind of Palladian bridge, Henry Flitcroft (1697–1769).

## 'By whose favour alone I am enabled to fill it' – Wilton bridge and the Rococo garden

It is likely that the idea for the 'Palladian' bridge at Wilton was Lord Pembroke's and that its practical realisation in elevations and groundplans came from Roger Morris. The pair had worked together on several projects in addition to the Victory Column at Blenheim, notably on the chaste Palladian proprieties of Marble Hill House, Twickenham, between 1724 and 1729. Their relationship architecturally was probably similar to that between Vanbrugh and Hawksmoor. A partnership of like minds can thrive when both parties accept their mutual indebtedness and enjoy it. Morris's descendants still own a silver cup presented by the Earl to Morris two years before they devised their bridge. It is inscribed 'Given by my Noble Patron Henry, Earl of Pembroke, by whose favour alone I am enabled to fill it. R. Morris 1734'.

Upon the Earl's succession in 1733 the pair had descended on the grounds of Wilton House like an aesthetic hurricane, transforming yet softening. The nature of a Rococo garden is not easy to describe and the name 'Rococo' is itself only half satisfactory because it conveys an air of things foreign with cherubs flitting on clouds and a prolixity of vapid curls. Yet the Rococo garden was an essentially English development and the origin of the 'Jardin Anglais' that was to take the fancy of half Europe before the century was out. Lord Burlington tends, with his Chiswick villa and London town house, to be associated with a rigid, even bloodless classicism yet his small park at Chiswick was, with its sudden surprise vistas crammed into a limited area and the

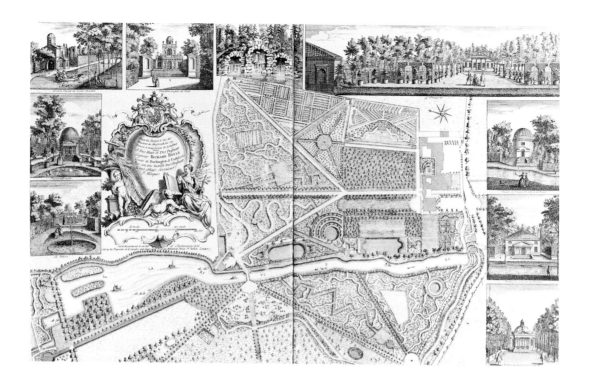

*Badeslade and Rocque's engraving, 1736, of the grounds at Chiswick illustrates the complex interrelation of the serpentine paths of the Rococo with the formal straight lines of the patte d'oie, the 'goose foot' of earlier garden layouts*

multiplicity of its architectural incidents and visual events – temples, rotonda, pyramid, obelisk and small lakes – a proto-Rococo layout.

What was added to gardens in the 1740s, the Rococo decade when Frederick, Prince of Wales, was setting the tone, was a more curvaceous and lightly feminine touch to the groves. The limited area, the abrupt surprise vistas remained while to Burlington's classical ornaments were added a whole range of foreign exotics – Moorish kiosks, Turkish *ombrellos*, Venetian seats, bark houses, hermits' caves, abbey and castle ruins in the inevitable Gothick. Perhaps the most influential current of this playful exoticism was the Chinese because it was accepted as a deliberate underwriting of the asymmetrical in a century of classical symmetry. And the most available and best loved of Chinese designs was that of the Willow Pattern plate with a high, quaint bridge central to its design and its legend.

The Wilton garden which the 9th Earl inherited was a typical, though decayed, formal layout of the 17th century, the Franco-Italian geometry that Inigo Jones and Isaac de Caus had created with the help of the French engraver Jacques Callot (1592–1635). The gardens' perspective, in the *Vitruvius Britannicus* of 1725, shows their rectangular outlines extending far beyond the Nadder and reaching with ruler-straight avenues up the further hillside. Virtually unnoticed, the Nadder itself meanders through the

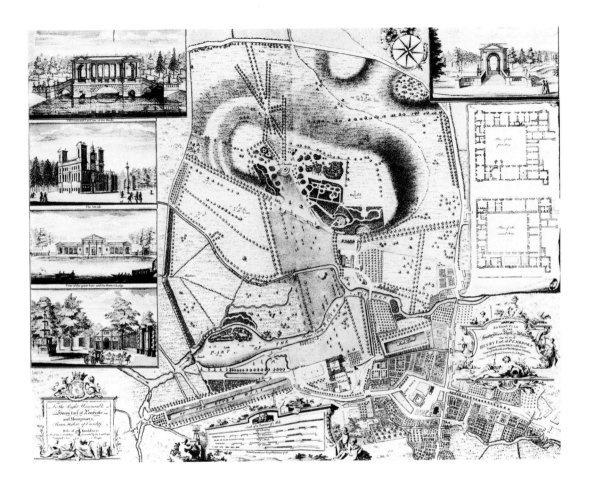

geometry. It had been one of the great gardens of England but the fashion for the paintings of Claude and Poussin had left it hopelessly old-fashioned.

Lord Pembroke believed, rightly as recent research has indicated, that the south front of Wilton House was a masterwork by his stylistic hero, Inigo Jones, not a design by the hydraulics engineer Isaac de Caus. So he added a bridge that Jones would have admired, then perversely set it in an asymmetrical and quite un-Jonesian Rococo garden.

By the time Rocque made his plan of the gardens in 1746 the transformation was almost complete. Two distinct gardens had been laid out. One near the house, and created around the new Palladian bridge, was a Rococo water garden, intricate with winding waterways and a lake where an Arcade dammed up the Nadder. The second was a Rococo woodland garden up on the hill, a place of sinuous rides and sudden asymmetrical clearings with a thatched house of rough bricks. Both the Arcade and the thatched house were sited to give views of Salisbury spire.

*Rocque's engraving, 1746, of Wilton park shows the remains of the earlier formal avenues still lying across the two separate Rococo gardens that the 9th Earl was creating. The Palladian bridge stands as an essential link between these two areas*

25

View of Wilton in Wiltshire the Seat of the R.t Hon.ble the Earl of PEMBROKE — Vüe de Wilton dans le Conté de Wilts &c. Maison & Jardin magnifique du Conte de PEMBROKE.

*Wilton House and the Palladian bridge in 1759. The Arcade can be seen at the far end of the new lake with Salisbury cathedral spire as a distant element in the composition framed between clumps of newly planted trees*

The connecting link between these two distinct gardens was the Palladian bridge. It was also the most prominent garden building in the views from the state rooms besides being the focus of several vistas within its own water garden. To appreciate how the Prior Park bridge was intended to function, an account of the Wilton bridge by John Loveday of Caversham in 1738 is illuminating:

> *In the Gardens (all laid open in the modern taste) is a serpentine River which runs with a good Current; over it this present Lord has erected a covered Bridge; 'tis a very light and most elegant Structure upon 5 rustic Arches; besides the beauty of it, this building serves two uses, that of a foot-bridge and that of a Summer-house on both sides the Water. You ascend the bridge by wide Stone Steps at the foot of which is an handsome Approach of Stone; the building is of the Ionic Order, under such an Arch you enter a square room, passed which you are in an oblong Space supported on each side by four Ionic Pillars, not Arches; at the other End of this Space is another square room; a Ballustrade of Stone (for such is the whole built of) runs on each side of the Lengths of the 3 Rooms. The roof is of brown Stucho in pannels, old Busts adorn the Inside and some Statues the Approach. The whole Structure is leaded.*

This means that the Palladian bridge was a water-cooled summer-house of three rooms. The Wilton designers took from Palladio's Rialto project the idea of the merchant's bourse with its cool open portico but realised it by opening out the smaller five-bay unit of the shops' outer elevation. They terminated their composition by cut-down versions of Palladio's end portico and swung the decorative mood down from the Corinthian to the Ionic order. That jaunty rise in the bridge's profile, the balustraded sides and the unpretentious scale that make the Herbert-Morris creation so captivating and light-hearted in its Rococo mood seem to have come from Lord Burlington's Scamozzi drawing, also for a Rialto project. This is now kept in the Burlington-Devonshire collection of the R.I.B.A. in London. No Palladio drawing of a bridge exists in that collection.

## 'Templa Quam Dilecta'
## – Stowe and the Palladian bridge as political symbol

Lord Pembroke was himself a sturdy Whig, First Lord of the Bedchamber and Groom of the Stole, but his allegiance was primarily to the reigning monarch George II and George, in so far as he cared to be a patron, was a first generation Palladian, not that second generation Palladian inclining to the Rococo. It was Lord Cobham who made Palladian bridges a sign of enlightened garden design among the 'boy patriots', that gang of dissident Whig politicians – the Temples, Lytteltons, Grenvilles and Pitts – who opposed the bland and pacific rule of Sir Robert Walpole and used Frederick, the Rococo Prince of Wales, as a focus for their political ambitions.

Cobham had been a highly successful soldier before turning to politics. He was no 'boy' himself, being 63 in 1733 when he began to lead a younger generation of ambitious men. By that time he had already begun the extraordinary group of park buildings that were to make the grounds of Stowe the most celebrated and visited in England, its fame extending later as far as Russia and St Petersburg. His family name was Temple, his motto was 'TEMPLA QUAM DILECTA' – How beautiful are thy temples – and he was an obsessive builder of park temples, each with an allegorical message of political significance. A favourite theme was the Whig party as natural heir to Saxon freedoms and liberty-loving Norman barons. By the time he came to a Palladian, or templar, bridge the message was – the British Empire.

News of the innovative bridge at Wilton would have reached him quickly. James Gibbs is most likely to have designed the close

replica of Lord Pembroke's creation that was in place by 1739 over
an arm of the Octagon Lake, out of sight of Stowe house. Gibbs
was the architect of all the other buildings that were going up at
this time in the Hawkwell Fields area of the park: the Temple of
Friendship (1739), the Gothic Temple (1741–4) and the Ladies'
Temple (1744–8).

As first designed the Stowe bridge had only a single colonnade on
its west side. The other was a blank wall decorated with paintings
of Sir Walter Raleigh and Sir William Penn by Francesco Sleter.
These flanked Scheemaker's sculptured relief of Britannia with the
four corners of the earth bringing her tribute – a tea house for the
imperially minded. In 1762 this 'imperial' wall was pulled down
and replaced by a second row of Ionic columns. Because it was
designed to take a carriage the Stowe bridge sits lower on the
water, compensating for its inferior profile by the heads of gods
and lions on its keystones where the Wilton bridge has only
acanthus or plain channels. Its link with the bridge at Prior Park
will be explored later.

## A decade of bridges – the 1740s

The 1740s were the high noon of the Rococo in England, that wave of stylistic fashion that never quite broke because the death of its arch-patron, Frederick, Prince of Wales, in 1751, disappointed all those eager politicians and architects who had been looking forward to pensions, patronage and positions when he became King Frederick I. But the 1740s at least were the decade for frivolous charm in garden design and for picturesque bridges arching up dramatically to link somewhere with nowhere.

At Dogmersfield, in Hampshire, Paulet St John built a Palladian bridge sited in true Willow Pattern composition over an arm of the Wale Pond near a group of thatched cottages and set about with trees. It was recorded by an artist about 1747 but vanished long ago. Lost too is the 'elegant bridge with a colonnade upon it' that Thomas Whately described in the Hon. George Grenville's park at Wotton in Buckinghamshire. It was designed by Sanderson Miller in 1758.

These more ephemeral temple bridges were probably made of wood. Palladio himself comes through his text as being more excited by the satisfying logic of wooden structures where he could work out his own solutions rather than relying on Roman precedent. Timber must have been the attraction for Henry Flitcroft or 'Burlington Harry' as he was known to his contemporaries.

Trained as a carpenter, the youthful Flitcroft had the good fortune to fall off scaffolding and break his leg while working on Burlington House in Piccadilly. Attracted by his plight and by his meticulous draughtsmanship Lord Burlington became his patron, securing his rise from Master Carpenter to Comptroller of the Office of Works. Breathing a rarefied Palladian air Flitcroft designed, among more important works, wooden bridges based closely on Palladio's Plate 5 in Book Three, at Ditchley Park, Oxfordshire, between 1736 and 1740, Stourhead in Wiltshire for Henry Hoare in 1749 and, most impressive of all, a 165-foot span across the new Virginia Water in Windsor Great Park for the Park Ranger, William Augustus, Duke of Cumberland, in about 1747.

Pure Palladian as that trio may have been (all are now perished) there is no doubt that they were seen in their time as Chinese by the high pitch of their arch and the angular patterns of their braces and *colonelli*. Hoare himself referred to Flitcroft's bridge as 'Chinese' in his letters and the Duke not only raised a Chinese pagoda on the banks of his lake but sailed its waters in a large Mandarin's yacht. Henry Hoare, in his later more neo-classical phase, added an authentic stone Palladian bridge to his lake, based on a mixture of Plates 7 and 12 in Palladio's Third Book.

William Etheridge designed and built a three-arched wooden bridge over the Thames at Walton between 1748 and 1750. Raised as a commercial venture it was approached by a stone causeway on 26 arches and was celebrated in its time, being twice painted by Canaletto and featured with an engraving in the *Gentleman's Magazine*. Though possibly conceived in the spirit of Palladian carpentry it bore no resemblance to any of Palladio's original designs. Etheridge went on to build a miniature version of it, with one arch only, over the Cam at Queen's College, Cambridge in 1749. This was rebuilt to Etheridge's design in 1902.

Somewhere between 1748 and 1754 an attractive templar bridge of at least some Palladian reference was built at Shugborough Park, Staffordshire, to carry the main drive from Stafford in over the lake. It had obelisks at its corners and an impertinent little temple perched over the central of its three arches. The great flood of 1795 swept away not only the bridge but the lake itself. Another vaguely Palladian essay of *c*1748 and possibly from the hand of Giovanni Niccolo Servandoni was drawn to cross a narrow arm of the lake at West Wycombe, Buckinghamshire. Servandoni was designing stage sets and stands for firework displays at the time and his West Wycombe bridge with a single wooden span and a two-storey domed pavilion at either end was a theatrical fantasy. Only a simple wooden bridge was ever built on the site.

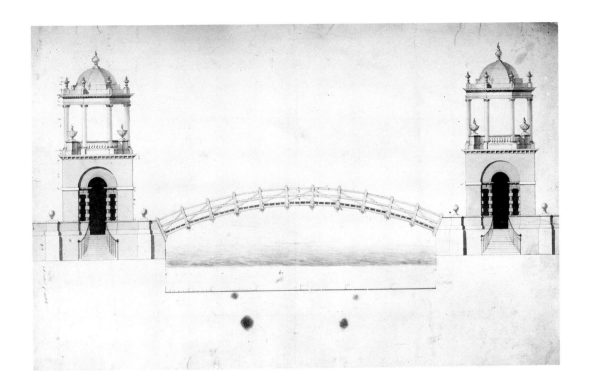

Meanwhile at Amesbury, a 17th-century classical house in Wiltshire, the more logical step had been taken and before 1748 a pavilion on a bridge 'after the Manner of the Chinese' had been created. This enchanting tea-house with its geometric joinery and patterns of flint flush-work still survives on an arch over a stream, 'an humble imitation of a Chinese house, which is well shaded and agreeable; but it consists only of one room, and is yet unfinished', to quote J. Hanway writing in 1757. It still has only one room but Sir William Chambers may have advised on its final form, its 'embellishing and Elegantifiing' in 1772. By its perverse symmetries the bridge house shows how easily the disciplines of the Roman and Chinese empires could be brought together to serve the same function.

*A design of c.1748 for a bridge at West Wycombe, attributed to Giovanni Servandoni (National Trust Photographic Library/Angelo Hornak)*

## 'The bridge over the pond'
## – the Prior Park bridge and William Pitt the Elder

Considering that the ornamental buildings of Prior Park were all erected in full view of a bustling resort-city, full of gossips and diarists, they are oddly anonymous. The reason for their obscurity is to be found in the nature of Ralph Allen, the creator of Prior

31

Park and of its landscape. Allen was essentially a *petit bourgeois* figure who rose to great wealth and political influence by his business skills and by his talent for cultivating the famous. He never wanted, like the Temples, to live in a palace; he only constructed one as a status symbol and as an advertisement for the stone and masonry that he could offer from his quarries and workshops up on Combe Down. Allen employed cheap local labour at every level, being quick to sack an architect like the elder John Wood when he felt that his own clerk of works, Richard Jones, could handle a building operation with less expense. It hardly mattered that 'the comfortless Palace of Prior Park' that Jones fitted up had only one room of any distinction and that a chapel. Allen and his wife lived in a modest apartment in one of the wings.

There is no mystery as to who actually constructed Allen's Palladian bridge or when the work took place. But to appreciate the motivation behind the construction of the bridge an understanding of the complex intermarriages of the 'boy patriots', that inner faction of the Whig party, is helpful.

Allen was a hard political animal. His first move to prosperity had been a spying operation on local Jacobites. A Whig for the influence and money, Allen shrewdly noted that rising Whig politicians were fixated on garden buildings as status symbols. With his own quarries and a captive workforce of masons Allen could turn out ambitious park buildings for himself at a quarter of the normal cost. His way of entertaining and flattering the influential was to take them out into his park, show off the latest building and then indulge them by asking for and sometimes taking their aesthetic advice. One consequence of that policy was a park crowded, in the Rococo fashion, with visual incidents that had very little relation to each other. There was money, there were buildings but there was no grand controlling plan or director of taste.

Allen's good fortune was that the 1750s were the years when the 'boy patriots' finally achieved power and military glory in the wars with France. Towering above the other 'patriots' was 'The Great Commoner', William Pitt the Elder. Here again Ralph Allen was lucky. His vast income from handling the postal system depended upon government favour. Pitt suffered agonies from hereditary gout and the pains could only be relieved by the hot waters of Bath. Consequently Pitt haunted the city. He had been MP for Old Sarum, Seaford, Aldborough and Okehampton, but for years he had been angling to be one of Bath's MPs and Bath was not a wholly 'rotten' borough; there would be an 'election' of a kind. Allen, notoriously the power behind Bath Corporation, would be a key figure in such an 'election', therefore the two men had a mutual interest in maintaining warm personal relations.

Pitt, never a wealthy man because he was too honest, loved gardens and was a keen amateur critic of architecture. His letters to Sanderson Miller, the gentleman architect of Radway in Warwickshire and a leading Goth, are particularly warm and affectionate. In one letter to Miller of 30th October 1755, Pitt wrote:

*I shall then have one call upon your Imagination for a very considerable Gothick Object which is to stand in a very fine situation on the Hills near Bath. It is for Mr Allen, the idea I will explain to you when we meet. The name of that excellent man will render my desires to you to do your best unnecessary. I shall have a particular pleasure in procuring to him the help of the Great Master of Gothick.*

It is on the strength of this letter that the Sham Castle on the hilltop above Bath has been attributed, wrongly, to Miller. But what matters is the date, 1755, Pitt's relationship with Allen, and the fact that in July 1757, after applying for the Chiltern Hundreds, Pitt became MP for Bath. It was in 1755 that the Palladian bridge was built in Prior Park. Was it then a product of the discreet play of interests passing between Pitt and Allen at that time?

*A page from the sketch book of Thomas Robins showing the eastern approach road to the bridge at Prior Park. The central pavilion and a turret of the east wing of the mansion are visible behind a Gothick temple and a maturing grove of trees (Conway Library, Courtauld Institute of Art)*

33

There exists in Bath City Library a rambling, cantankerous document entitled *The Life of Richard Jones*. It is a transcript of dictation taken down from Allen's long-serving and suffering clerk of works when the old man was near to death. At one point the narration breaks off inconsequentially from an account of Allen's tree planting to state, baldly:

> *In the year 1755 he ordered me to build the bridge over the pond; the foundation stone was laid by Mr Allen May 29th, 1755.*

At no point does Jones praise the bridge or claim that he designed it. He states twice, however, that the Sham Castle was 'to my plan' and 'to my design', only grumbling that he would have built it larger 'but was hindered by my master and other gentlemen'. It can, therefore, be accepted that Jones did not design the bridge.

To consider further who might have designed the Palladian bridge that Jones clearly constructed it is necessary to venture into the complex family relationships of the 'boy patriots'.

Lord Cobham, their founder, had given William Pitt his first paid employment, a cornetcy in Lord Cobham's Horse, 'The King's Own', and Cobham had been quick himself to build a copy of the Wilton bridge at Stowe, making it a symbol of Britain's imperial destiny. The other leading 'boy patriots' were George Lyttelton, George and Richard Grenville, the Pelhams and, of course, William Pitt himself. Both George Lyttelton, later Lord Lyttelton of Frankley, and George Grenville built Palladian bridges – Lyttelton at Hagley, his Worcestershire seat, and Grenville at Wotton. Lyttelton had been secretary to Frederick, Prince of Wales. Hagley had riotous Rococo plasterwork and the park was the epitome of Rococo indulgence with urns to Pope and Shenstone, a castle, a rotonda, a column to the Prince of Wales, a hermitage, a grotto, a cascade, seats to Thomson and Milton and a statue of Venus. George Lyttelton's mother was Christian Temple, Lord Cobham's sister. Rococo garden buildings ran in families. George Grenville's park at Wotton had a similar eclectic array and his mother Hester was another of Lord Cobham's sisters. She would inherit her brother's viscountcy by special dispensation after his death in 1749.

That is not the end of the interrelations. George and Richard Grenville also had a sister and her name also was Hester. She married William Pitt in 1754, making another loop in the Palladian knot of connections. Finally Pitt himself had a nephew, Thomas Pitt, later 1st Lord Camelford, and Thomas Pitt was the gifted amateur architect who was to design in 1764 the Palladian bridge at Hagley for George Lyttelton. Thomas Pitt is now an almost

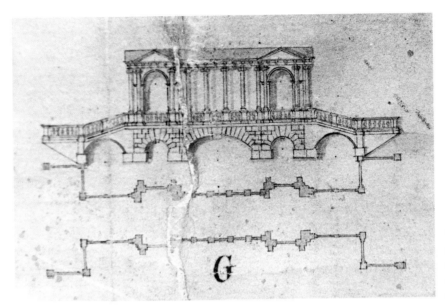

forgotten figure but in his lectures Sir John Soane rated him alongside Lords Burlington and Pembroke as a leader of English architectural taste. Thomas Pitt and Sanderson Miller were equally devoted to William Pitt. In 1779 Miller set up a memorial urn that Thomas Pitt had sent him from Bath, placing it under a grove of trees that William Pitt had planted at Radway in 1754.

While the evidence is not conclusive, anyone who has read through this maze of relationships will agree that Ralph Allen probably built the Prior Park bridge on the advice of, and to flatter, William Pitt and that Thomas Pitt is most likely to have designed the bridge that Richard Jones constructed.

This most happily sited of all Palladian bridges composes superbly with the great house hunched above it on the skyline, Prior Park's wings being mercifully hidden by trees. The interval between the central columns of the bridge is wider than the other five bays. On the meticulously drawn illustration of the bridge on Thorp and Overton's map *Survey of the Manours* of 1761 all the five intervals are regular, so perhaps Richard Jones left one small mark on the work. From the house itself the bridge is almost lost in greenery. Allen as usual was more interested in impressing visitors than in indulging himself.

## 'J'aime à la folie les jardins à l'anglaise'
## – Catherine's Palladian bridge at Tsarskoe Selo

In 1771, persuaded by her lover, Stanislaus Poniatowski, who had greatly admired the gardens at Stowe, Catherine the Great,

Empress of Russia, sent the Russian architect Vasily Neelov to study English architecture and landscape. He returned to St Petersburg with the Hanoverian John Busch to landscape a section of the park of Tsarskoe Selo and build the Empress a Palladian bridge over a channel of a Rococo water maze. The bridge was completed in 1774. It is simpler than the Wilton bridge, there are no keystones to its rusticated arches but it is far more imperial in its materials. The rustication is executed in pink granite, the steps are of white marble and the columns with their entablature are composed of blue-grey Siberian marble.

Catherine may have seen the illustration of the Wilton bridge in the volume of *Vitruvius Britannicus* that was published in 1771. Her Tsarskoe bridge represents Russia in a cultural stage similar to that of the USA in the last half of the 19th century – a rich new power eager to acquire the trappings of older and more sophisticated countries, confident that 'whatever they can do, we can do better'.

After suffering some damage in the German siege of Leningrad the bridge has been restored to its original condition and sometimes serves as a summer lido for day-trippers.


## The last bridges

When Neelov was building the bridge at Tsarskoe Selo the Wilton design had ceased to be either a novelty or a political symbol in England. Thomas Pitt's bridge at Hagley appears to have been the last true replica and may well have been of timber construction, hence its subsequent disappearance. But the notion of a monumental temple linking two shores was too poetic ever to be abandoned.

Already in 1773 Capability Brown was updating the form with an elegant tea-house on a three arched bridge in the park at Scampston Hall in the East Riding of Yorkshire. Its slim Ionic columns are paired and, like the first state of the Stowe bridge, its rear wall is blank to provide shelter from wind and rain. The attenuation of later Regency neo-Classicism is already foreshadowed and when Robert Adam designed a summer-house on a bridge close to the cascade at Audley End, Essex, in 1783, he produced a building very close to the Scampston tea-house.

But these were slight ornaments. The memory of Palladio's Rialto project haunted the ambitions of architects as Britain became a global power and its rulers hankered after monumental structures to match the empire they controlled. In 1771 Thomas Sandby exhibited 'The Bridge of Magnificence' at the Royal Academy. This splendid monster was to have projected from the middle of Somerset House, crossing the Thames on seven arches

with a domed palace at each end and something like the
Clarendon Building in Oxford perched in the middle. Inevitably
John Soane with the fantasist Joseph Gandy in support out-
trumped Sandby with titanic bridge palaces in the various classical
orders that would have blocked the Thames at Vauxhall and
accommodated all departments of Government and the Royal
family for the next hundred years.

*Pulteney Bridge, Bath, designed by Robert Adam and completed by 1774. Thomas Malton's view of 1785 illustrates what is perhaps the best realisation of Andrea Palladio's original vision of a monumental city bridge with shops*

Much later, in the fading years of the imperial dream, Edwin Lutyens produced a gallery bridge to span the modest Liffey in Dublin. Like the Wilton bridge it would have had a colonnaded centre, but of seven bays with a domed temple at each end to accommodate, with maximum inconvenience, the paintings of Sir Hugh Lane's controversial bequest.

Yet one monumental version of Palladio's failed scheme did get built and has become so much an accepted feature of the Bath street scene that it tends to be taken for granted. This is the bridge that William Pulteney, a Bath developer, persuaded his friend Robert Adam to design in order to link the city's shops to the high class residential estate on Bathwick that he was planning. An Act of Parliament gave permission for such a bridge in 1768, Bath Corporation gave their consent in 1769 and by 1774 the bridge was built, bankrupting only Reed, its contractor. The way was open for the tremendous Prussian-style avenue of Pulteney Street with the houses Adam may have hoped to design but which the Bath architect Thomas Baldwin deviously took over from him. Five radiating avenues had originally been planned. For even one to be carried out on such a scale was superbly un-English.

If Adam's bridge has a fault it is its lack of transparency, the basic Palladian quality. No one who crosses the bridge is aware of the river. But from downstream the effect is impressive with a perverse union of lower strength in the sparsely decorated arches and a frail upper elegance of two shallow domes and five thin pediments. Above the roaring V of the weirs and the sinister brown waters of the Avon, Andrea Palladio's ambition 'to keep up the grandeur and dignity of the said city, and also to add a very great income to it', has been achieved at least in part.